Handmade By God

Heidi Ruth Shirra

GILEAD
BOOKS

First published in Great Britain by Gilead Books Publishing, June 2012, reprinted 2021
2 4 6 8 10 9 7 5 3

www.GileadBooksPublishing.com

British Library Cataloguing-in-Publication Data:
A catalogue record for this book is available from the British Library.
ISBN-13: 978-0-9568560-4-3

Photography: Oliver Shirra

My hope is in you, so may
goodness and honesty guard me.

Psalm 25:21 (NCV)

My Journey so far...

My name is Heidi, 5ft5, 21 years old, enjoy dancing, lying in at weekends and having a drink at the pub with friends on Fridays, so pretty normal, but I've come to learn that there is no 'normal' when it comes to life.

When I was 18 I faced the daunting decision of what to do with my life. I could go to university and get a degree, go on to have a well paid job, marry the man of my dreams, live in a wonderful Victorian house and have lots of children. Of course there was always the other option of stepping straight into the big wide world to find a job. This option was tempting: no more studying, earning my own money, but as my parents were quick to point out, it's hard work. University is a once in a lifetime experience and why would I want to miss out on that? So, needless to say, I took the more appealing option and I decided to go to university.

I was leaning towards studying teaching, having always loved children and completed work experience in a primary school. I researched the qualifications you would need and tailored my A'levels to ensure I would be eligible to apply. After a while I found myself wondering if I really wanted to spend my life in a 'sensible' job. I had always loved dancing, both performing and in church, and thought I was quite good (if I do say so myself). At the last minute I changed my mind and went for dancing, a more risky option perhaps but, I thought, what better than to spend three years doing what I love? Thankfully I passed all 4 subjects and got the grades I needed. I was in, I was going to university!

I had chosen the University of Lincoln. It was just an hour away from home and where my grandparents and auntie lived. Coincidentally, I was born there and had moved away when I was four, so it was a home from home really. I was excited about going but naturally a little apprehensive too. I've always been a bit of a home-bird, but after a day trip to IKEA with my mum, the idea of moving away seemed much more appealing.

So off I went. My room was bare at first but I soon brightened it up. Of course there were a few initial teething problems (like the fact that we had no hot water for the first day) but the fact that we were all in it together made it seem nothing more than funny. My classes were intense and often lasted up to three hours each plus essays and performances, but I thoroughly enjoyed them. On my course I made friends with three girls in particular. The first, Donna, lived in the block of apartments next door and we spent most our time together, walking to class, doing homework together, giggling about classes in the cafe next to the studio. I soon found out that Donna was a Christian and I felt I could talk to her about more than just dancing. After a month or two I joined the Christian Union and so we went along together. Not long afterwards another friend Becca started to come too. I would go to church on Sundays and I admit that I felt that God had truly placed me there.

When I first started university I was dating a guy who lived in the Lake District (a 4 hour train journey). I would take my luggage to my last lecture on the Thursday afternoon, run to the train station and then spend the evening changing trains and would arrive there late evening. After the weekend I would head back on the Sunday night and do my class work on the train before starting back again on the Monday. So I kept myself busy!

As lovely as this boyfriend was, he was becoming increasingly demanding and obsessive about knowing where I was and when, and my feelings for him soon faded. After a messy break-up, we finished in the February. During September to February, I hadn't noticed at the time, but I was slowly losing weight. When I went home for weekends my mum would comment, but I wouldn't take any notice. Unbeknownst to me, I had started developing the first signs of an eating disorder. I became fussy about the type of foods that I ate and determined to eat a more healthy diet and 'cut out the junk'.

During my time at university I became very self critical and unhappy with the reflection I saw in the mirror. You see, dancing for 5 hours a day in front of a mirror in skin tight clothing, I was forced to look at what I saw as my flaws and imperfections, and I became dissatisfied. My mum was a personal trainer and I was well aware of what I should be eating and how to eat in a healthy manner, but I abused this knowledge and decided to go on a diet, just to 'lose a few wobbly bits'. At this point I was around a dress size 8/10.

So I began to eat less, but after I'd mastered eating a certain amount of food, it then started to seem too much, even greedy. So I decided to eat a little less and see how I managed, and so the pattern continued. It wasn't long before it started to affect my dancing. I would become dizzy and feel faint and before long I was sitting out in every class. I went to the doctors to try and figure out 'the problem' but of course they never found a solution. Naively I thought that what I was doing wasn't affecting my health or ability to function. But even carrying the food shopping home from town was becoming a struggle.

When I went home for weekends I noticed that I would feel irritable if I couldn't exercise. I wasn't comfortable eating the same foods as I had done previously. I had become used to doing as I pleased and preparing my own food, I didn't like the idea of others doing my cooking and dictating what I ate or watching me at dinner. Eating was no longer fun, enjoyable or sociable; it was a controlled operation to be completed in solitary confinement.

By the time summer arrived and the university term year finished, I found I was in more trouble than I thought. I had slowly lost weight throughout the year and was fully immersed in a world of counting calories and exercise; nothing else mattered. During the summer I ate less and less and spent my days either lying on the sofa zapped of energy or walking for hours at a time. My life was ruled by what had now become an eating disorder. I was now smaller than a size 6 and frequently found myself buying children's clothes. Shopping was no longer fun and I hated going out in case I was challenged with the scary prospect of food.

Of course my parents realized what was happening. Unbeknownst to me I was suffering from body dysmorphia and the reflection I saw in the mirror was far from the reality of my ever-decreasing frame. My parents took me to the doctor where I was weighed and simply told to eat more. Of course things were never going to be that simple. I lied to my parents about what I was eating and how long I had been exercising for. I lived a life of secrecy. I couldn't trust anyone and I became withdrawn and depressed. I had countless visits to the doctor and was always told I wasn't 'ill enough' to receive any treatment.

In a desperate attempt to help me, my parents paid for me to visit a counsellor once a week. She was kind and understanding and listened to what I had to say without getting upset or angry at me. She helped take the strain off my parents and helped me to explore the possible motives behind my behaviour and really express how I was feeling. After a few months I began to accept that I was suffering from anorexia, although to this day I still hate that word. After another reluctant visit to the doctor, I agreed to be monitored by a nurse and have regular blood tests. I also agreed to attempt to eat more food to prevent losing any more weight. I was informed by my doctor on this visit that I shouldn't return to university next year until I was eating more. I remember breaking down in tears in the doctor's surgery. I couldn't imagine not returning to Lincoln, being left behind and losing my friends and the life I had built for myself there.

During the remainder of the summer I battled to eat more food, week by week increasing the amount. The side effects were terrible and at times I couldn't bear the sight of food, but slowly I managed to increase my intake.

It got easier but it got to August and I was still not eating enough. It was a heart-breaking time for me: I had tried so hard, and all my work had gone to waste. I had to stay at home.

During this time my grandad's health had deteriorated. He was suffering with terminal cancer which put extra pressure on my parents and added to my anxiety. We all went on holiday to Cornwall, knowing it would be his last, when he became jaundiced and had to return home early. He was quickly admitted into hospital and it soon became clear he wasn't going to get any better. My mum and I had taken a day trip up to visit him. During our visit we were informed that he was suffering with multiple organ failure and declining fast. Over the next week I couldn't bring myself to leave him and go home, so I stayed sometimes through the night, and before long he was gone from my life forever. My grandad was a very special person in my life and his loss was hard to overcome.

During this difficult time my eating had taken a back seat and I had slipped back to my old habits. I was still eating but not as well as I had been. I got myself a part time job as a waitress and studied for a couple of evening classes which kept me busy and gave me a focus, something to work towards. By the time next September came around I decided that dance wasn't for me anymore; I was already behind by a year and I needed a fresh start.

I passed my exams and came out with a diploma in body massage and a certificate in reflexology studies. I had really enjoyed learning about the body and discovered a passion for anatomy. I looked at various jobs and after months of applying got a job in a hospital as a physiotherapy assistant. I thrived working in the hospital environment and loved working with patients.

So that was 2009 and now it's 2012. During these last few years I tried a lot of things to help my recovery and one thing that did work was writing. I would look up an inspirational bible verse, and write down what it meant to me. I'd pin them up in my room and every time I saw them they would give me a boost. This book is composed of some of those bible verses and my thoughts on them. I wanted to share them in the hope that they may help you as they did me.

In the last three years I've still had my ups and downs but the support I have received from the people around me has been invaluable. During this time I have come to learn that there are so many people around me struggling with not only eating disorders but low self esteem, depression and other mental and physical conditions. Our lives should not be dictated by these problems and nor should we have to put up with them. God made us by hand, he made a plan for our lives and he wants us to live it to the full. Three years ago I wasn't living my life to the full, but I can safely say that now I am, God has healed me from my illness and with His grace I am learning to love myself again and be the person he made me to be.

The selection of bible verses in this book helped me get through the toughest days. Read one verse a week, one a day, or whenever you need encouragement and motivation to get through the day. The space at the bottom of the page is for your own notes as you reflect on how wonderfully you are made and loved, hand crafted by God.

Heidi

Before I formed you in the womb I knew you, before you were born I set you apart; I appointed you as a prophet to the nations.

Jeremiah 1:5 (NIV)

I was handmade by God. He hand-picked everything about me, and he loves everything about me. Every part of me was specifically made and that makes me unique, one of a kind. There is no-one else in the world the same as me and that makes me special.

We should never feel inadequate, because God has provided us with the tools and skills that we need for our lives and for his work.

So we should feel secure and confident that we were made perfectly for the life God has planned for us, and he loves us just the way we are.

I urge you to pray for absolutely everything.
Mark 11:25 (TM)

When we find ourselves struggling, God tells us to pray. This may sound simple, but it can be surprising how often we can forget to pray. God doesn't want us to just ask for help for the big problems, but for all our problems, no matter how big or small.

So remember to turn to God in every circumstance, because there is no problem too big or small for him to resolve.

The Lord is my helper; I will not be afraid. What can mere mortals do to me?

Hebrews 13:6 (NIV)

If I were to ask who scares you, what would you say; your dad, your boss, perhaps a group of lads that hang around near the shop...or God? Fearing God doesn't fit with the all loving, and caring God we know. But God is powerful, he can command the sea, and turn a woman into a tower of salt, can your boss do that? My point is that although we encounter people in life that can intimidate us, what they are able to do to us is nothing compared to God's protection.

When we feel scared, worried or intimidated remember that we have a God that is bigger than they are, he can protect us and is more powerful than anyone on earth.

Having hope will give you courage.
Job 11:18 (NLT)

Job taught us that when we have hope, we have courage. I have often found myself in situations where I dare not hope for too much at the risk of feeling let down or getting hurt. However, God tells us that the hope we have in him is a certainty, because he can do anything.

We can feel sure of God's ability to fulfil our biggest hopes and have courage to go and live life to the full. God can help us do the things we want to do, therefore hope and God will fulfil.

It's in Christ that we find out who we are.

Ephesians 1:11 (TM)

This may seem an odd statement, and you may think you know who you are. But what the bible is saying here is that it is important to find out who God made us to be, only then will we know our creator's true intentions for ourselves. So how do we do that? Simple: pray.

Pray that God may enter our life, put him in control and ask him to show us the way. It may not be apparent right away, but he is desperate to show us what he made us to be. So what are we waiting for?

Let us strip off every weight that slows us down, especially the sin that so easily trips us up. And let us run with endurance the race God has set before us.

Hebrews 12:1 (NLT)

Sin is something no-one likes to talk about, but it's unavoidable. Sin can often hold us back from doing the things we want to do, or play on our minds and pull us down. We all sin, but the difference when you're a Christian is that you can ask God to wash it away.

So remember when something is holding us back, ask God to wash it away. We don't need to live life with sin weighing us down.

Now faith is being sure of what we hope for and certain of what we do not see.

Hebrews 11:1 (NIV)

It is a common misconception that being a Christian is easy, its not, it can be really hard. It means putting our trust and faith in the hands of God and his plan for us.

We don't know what will happen in our lives, but God does, so we trust him. It's not called having a faith for nothing.

Do not be shaped by this world; instead be changed within by a new way of thinking. Then you will be able to decide what God wants for you; you will know what is good and pleasing to him and what is perfect.

Romans 12:1-2 (NCV)

God has a plan for each of us. He knows us inside out and he wants to lead us into the best life possible. It can be easy to be sucked into worldly wants and desires and forget that we have a God who loves us, cares for us and knows what is best for us. God promises that if we trust in him, he will show us the way, the truth and a life that is pleasing and perfect to him.

Do not worry about our life, instead, put it in the hands of God and he will lead us.

I will be with you always, even until the end of this age.

Matthew 28:20 (NCV)

We can often feel lonely, helpless and in need of comfort and help. But God knows all my deepest thoughts and troubles and will always be with me. No matter where I go, what I do and however hard life gets, he promises to never leave me.

He can help us out of the hardest of times and restore us to our full glory.

And we know that God causes everything to work together for the good of those who love God and are called according to his purpose for them.

Romans 8:28 (NLT)

When something doesn't turn out the way we want, it can be disappointing. God tells us that everything works out the way he wanted and he has our best interests at heart. So although it may not be what we would have planned, it's the way he wanted it. God has a purpose for each of us and his plans reflect this.

As we look at our lives we will see all the ways God has used us and the gifts and talents he has given us. He gave us them for a reason and he will use them.

Trust in the Lord with all your heart,
and lean not on your own understanding;
in all your ways acknowledge him,
and he will make your paths straight.
Proverbs 3:5-6 (NIV)

Often we can find ourselves feeling lost and confused, not knowing where to go and what to do.

However, God tells us that when we completely trust in him, he will set our paths straight. This means he will show us the way and guide us where he wants and needs us to go.

It can be easy to try and plan our own lives, but God knows best, so try and take life step by step, letting God lead us.

You become the slave of whatever you choose to obey.

Romans 6:16 (NLT)

Let us fix our eyes on Jesus.

Hebrews 12:12 (NIV)

God tells us to obey him, to make sure he is the most important thing in our lives and ensure that nothing is of a higher importance than him.

However, sometimes we do put things above God, even without realising. As we do this, we begin to become a slave to it, and it can take over a part of who we are. Ensure we keep our eyes fixed on God and welcome him to be the most important part of us.

LORD, you are my hope. LORD, I have trusted you since I was young.

Psalm 71:5 (NCV)

Think back to when you were a child and how easy it was to trust people, we had to rely on others to survive.

However, as we grow older we become more independent and can get into the habit of 'going it alone', and by doing this we can grow independent from God. It is important to remember that we are still a child of God and we have an Almighty Father to care for us and guide us, try to trust God like we did as a child.

Even perfection has its limits.

Psalm 119:96 (NLT)

Perfection is an unachievable goal. Striving to do our best is good, but it is important that we allow ourselves to make mistakes and embrace our faults and failures.

Our faults and failures help us to learn, grow and strengthen as Christians and determine our uniqueness. God doesn't expect us to be perfect and faultless all the time, and so neither should I. So have reasonable expectations and allow yourself to enjoy life and its little hiccups.

Do not worry about tomorrow.
Matthew 6:34 (NKJV)

It is easy to become wrapped up in worry and stress about life, what is to come next and how we might cope.

However, God does not want us to worry, he says we should give our worries to him and he will show us the way. So next time we find ourselves worrying about tomorrow, concentrate on today, enjoy it, and cherish every moment of the life that God has given us. It would be a waste to worry life away.

Cease from anger...it only causes harm.

Psalm 37:8 (NKJV)

Anger is a natural emotion and we all feel it from time to time, it's almost unavoidable. What this bible verse is saying is that we shouldn't remain angry, because this is when we can harm people.

Next time you feel angry, take a moment, decide to let the anger go, then give the situation to God.

Don't let anger ruin your day; rise above it knowing God is with us always, through the ups and downs.

He will take care of you.

Psalm 55:22 (NLT)

It is not uncommon to feel alone, especially in situations where we need help. However God tells us we are never alone. He is always with us, guiding, supporting and caring for us every minute of every day.

The next time you feel alone, ask God to take care of you and feel comforted in the knowledge that he is always by our side.

Praise be to the God and Father of our Lord Jesus Christ, the Father of compassion and the God of all comfort.

2 Corinthians 1:3 (NIV)

At times we need to be supported, at times we need to be listened to, and sometimes we need someone to be compassionate to us and comfort us. God provides us with everything we need, including comfort.

Today go out knowing that in every situation, God is there for us, compassionate and waiting to listen.

Your kingdom come, your will be done.
Matthew 6:10 (NKJV)

We pray the Lord's Prayer often, but do we ever stop to consider what each line is saying?

When we say the Lord's Prayer, we are asking for God's will to be done. This means that we need to accept that God does have a plan for us, he can see the bigger picture, and he knows what is best for us, after all he did make us.

So it is important to avoid being discouraged if things don't go our way, because they have probably gone God's way instead.

There is a time to gain, and a time to lose.

Ecclesiastes 3:6 (NKJV)

At some point in our lives, it is likely that we will lose something. It may be our job, our health, our finances or a loved one. At these times we can often feel hopeless and struggle to find our way. In these situations the bible tells us that the Lord can make a new beginning out of an ending.

So trust the Lord because he knows our thoughts, fears and struggles, and let him transform us and lead us towards a new life he has already created for us.

So my dear brothers and sisters, stand strong. Do not let anything move you. Always give yourselves fully to the work of the Lord, because you know that your work in the Lord is never wasted.

1 Corinthians 15:58 (NCV)

When we feel like giving up and quitting, it can be hard to motivate ourselves. But we shouldn't let anything get in the way of God's plan for us, he wants what is best for us and so should we.

So persevere and remember God will equip us with all the skills we need to do his work. He is always with us, cheering us on. He is our biggest fan.

A happy heart is like good medicine, but a broken spirit drains your strength.

Proverbs 17:22 (NCV)

There is an old saying that 'laughter is the best medicine'. I bet you didn't realise its origin is from this verse in the bible. Try to approach each day as a fresh start, focusing on the positives instead of the negatives. You may be surprised how uplifting it can be.

And remember, there is always a reason to rejoice and be happy, because we are saved and have the everlasting love from God.

Lift up your eyes on high, and see who has created these things.

Isaiah 40:26 (NKJV)

Everyone has days when we feel uninspired. On the days when we lack motivation, look not only to God for encouragement, but to his creation that surrounds us.

Everything we can see, he has made. And the handmade world that we live in is beautiful and truly inspiring. Try to see God in all you do, and do everything for God.

The Lord disciplines those he loves, and he punishes everyone he accepts as his child.
Hebrews 12:6 (NCV)

This verse may sound severe; surely God is an all loving God? He is. However, we often forget that God is our father and like a father, he needs to discipline his children. This is for our benefit so that we may know what is right and wrong, and to build up our strength and understanding. In these times it is important to understand our mistake and make a decision to change and move on. But don't be discouraged, these times will strengthen and prepare us to be the disciples he needs us to be.

Your Father knows what you need before you ask.

Mathew 6:8 (CEV)

We have a creator, he knows us inside out and upside down. He knows everything about our life, what our school grades will be, what job we will have, who we will marry, and this means he knows exactly what we need. There is no harm in asking God to provide for us what we will need, but there is no point in worrying that we will be left short. God has a plan for us and he will equip us with everything we need to fulfil that plan.

So don't worry about having enough, simply trust in our creator and look forward to all the wonderful things he has planned for us and the gifts he will give us along the way.

God has also given each of us different gifts to use.

Romans 12:6 (CEV)

When God created us, he gave us each gifts. Each of these gifts is special to us, and we all have them. They are not the same gifts, which is why some people are good at listening, some are good at speaking to large crowds, some are gifted at dancing, music, creating, whatever the gift, God gave it to us. We need to discover our gifts and use them to glorify Him.

Do not be jealous that someone else can do something better, just remember we have our own gift from God, and that makes us unique.

We are not saying that we can do this work ourselves. It is God who makes us able to do all that we do.

2 Corinthians 3:5 (NCV)

When people say I am 'doing Gods work', what they really mean is, 'I am doing what God has asked me to do'. Within Gods plan, he uses every single one of us to do his work, and we need to have the confidence to do what God asks.

There are times in our lives when we can often feel inadequate, inexperienced or perhaps under qualified. However, when we are part of God's plan, he equips us with all the skills and ability we need.

So don't shy away, be confident and feel secure that God provides us with everything we need.

See how very much our Father loves us, for he calls us his children, and that is what we are! But the people who belong to this world don't recognize that we are God's children because they don't know him.

1 John 3:1 (NLT)

We are God's children and he is our Father. That means he loves us as a father loves a child. He made us to be unique, special, individual, beautiful and perfect just as we are. He wouldn't change one thing about us, not one.

However, we can often be critical about ourselves and can't see what God can see. He handmade us and he loves everything about us, we are perfect in his eyes. So let's try and look at ourselves the way God can see us, unique, wonderful and beautiful.

Forgetting the past and looking forward to what lies ahead.

Philippians 3:13 (NLT)

Some people say that our past dictates who we become, however this is not how God tells us to live our lives. When we accept him into our lives, he wipes away mistakes from our past and gives a new, fresh life to live.

There is no need to let our past dictate who we are, but rather look forward to the new life God has for us.

Use the gift you have.

1 Timothy 4:14 (NCV)

God gives us all special gifts, but they are not given to just to look at, they are given so that we can use them. When we use our God given talents, they bring glory to Him. So let's try and focus on what we can do, not what we can't do. Look around at all the people in our lives who have special talents. Have confidence that God gave a particular gift to us, and don't be afraid to use it and shine.

His sheep follow him because they know his voice.

John 10:4 (NIV)

When we pick up the phone, we can usually tell who it is, because we recognise their voice. However we sometimes struggle to hear God's voice. It is important for us to have a strong relationship with God, and the way to do that is to spend time with Him.

Try to set aside time to get to know God. That way, when he speaks, we will recognise his voice.

Their weakness was turned to strength.

Hebrews 11:34 (NLT)

We can often find ourselves worrying about our weaknesses and the things we can't do. But God can transform them into our strengths to be used for his glory. For example; if we feel we are shy, God can use us to talk to people who feel out of the group.

God will use our weaknesses and transform us into a strong person who is not afraid to do his work, so don't worry about our weaknesses, instead let God use them.

We know that God is always at work for the good of everyone who loves him. They are the ones God has chosen for his purpose.

Romans 8:28 (CEV)

God designed you for a purpose; he chose you and made an extraordinary plan for your life. So today, know that you have a purpose and God has the plan, all you need to do is ask him for the directions.

But I say to you, love your enemies. Pray for those who hurt you.

Matthew 5:44 (NCV)

This is a well known, yet odd sounding quote from the bible. Love those who hurt you...why?

Well God wants us to love everyone like he loves them, anyone can love the most lovable people but it takes a special person to love those who are not always so friendly.

If we manage to pray for those who hurt us, this means that you no longer need to let that person hurt you. God will look after them and their life; you need to get on with yours.

So don't be brought down by the people who hurt you, pray for them and move on with God's marvellous plan for you.

I was very worried, but you comforted me and made me happy.

Psalm 94:19 (NCV)

God is the greatest comforter in the world. If we are worried, he should be the first person we turn to. He knows our inner thoughts and feelings, he knows what has happened and what will happen and he can comfort us in even the most distressing situations.

Next time you begin to worry, turn to Him and he will comfort you.

He washed away our sins, giving us a new birth and new life through the Holy Spirit.

Titus 3:5 (NLT)

When we accept Jesus into our lives, he washes away our sins and makes us clean again. Don't let past mistakes tarnish your new beginning, thank God for taking them away and live your life to the full.

I know how to live on almost nothing or with everything. I have learned the secret of living in every situation.

Philippians 4:11-13 (NLT)

Everyone has their home comforts, things we 'can't live without'. However, the bible tells us that all we need is God and faith in Him. With Him on our side, we can tackle every situation no matter how much or how little we have.

Today, remember you are on the winning side, God's side.

Fix your thoughts on what is true, and honourable and right, and pure, and lovely and admirable.

Philippians 4:8 (NLT)

Our thoughts affect how we feel, think and act. When we think positively we will have a more positive attitude and therefore act in a positive way.

Today, ensure you fill your mind with positive, inspiring and encouraging thoughts as this is how God wants us to live.

You made all the delicate, inner parts of my body and knit me together in my mothers womb.

Psalm 139:13 (NLT)

When you look in the mirror what do you see?

God made every intricate detail of you intentionally, he knit you together by hand and he loves every single part of you, inside and out.

Today, when you look in a mirror, see a hand-crafted and perfect being that God has made and loves.

Wait for the LORD; be strong and take heart and wait for the LORD.

Psalm 27:14 (NIV)

In life we are used to having things at the click of a button, you could say we are not used to waiting for things to happen, but this is where God is different.

God has a plan for us and he knows what is best for us and he will guide us in our lives if we ask, but he will do it in his time. God's timing is perfect, so even though it may be frustrating to wait, be patient and remember he won't forget, he is just waiting for the perfect moment.

Don't be afraid; just believe.

Mark 5:36 (NIV)

Fear is an emotion most of us have felt, and it can prevent us from doing things we want to. There is no need for us to live in fear, that's not living life to the full. I'm not saying that as a Christian you won't feel afraid, you will, its part of life, but you can learn to trust God and to turn to him for protection and comfort.

To fully live out the plan God has for us, we have to believe and trust him. Life may be scary but with God you can be sure that you won't be afraid for long. Next time you feel afraid, stop and pray and feel the relief and comfort of God's protection.

For the Lamb on the throne will be their Shepherd. He will lead them to springs of life-giving water. And God will wipe every tear from their eyes.

Revelation 7:17 (NLT)

God acts as our guide, like our own shepherd, and he has amazing plans for our life. It can be easy to think we know what's best for us, but the reality is, God knows best. God can see things we can't see, he knows the things in our life that will trip us up, let us down and he knows the best route for our life.

We can learn to turn to him to lead us through our life, all we need to do is ask and enjoy the journey.

Give all your worries and cares to God, for he cares about you.

1 Peter 5:7 (NLT)

There is a common saying 'worrying wont get you anywhere' and its true, but it doesn't stop us from worrying. God asks us to give our worries and cares to him because he has the solutions.

God knows how you feel and cares about you, next time you realize you are worrying, ask God to take your worries away.

If anyone thirsts, let him come to me and drink. Rivers of living water will brim and spill out of the depths of anyone who believes in me this way, just as the Scripture says.

John 7:37 (TM)

Jesus says, if we are thirsty we should come to him and he will quench our thirst.

What I think he means is, if we are in need he will provide. Often we find ourselves in need of support, encouragement, motivation, self control etc. and it can be easy to forget that we have a God who will provide us with these things that we need. He even goes as far to say that he will make us overflowing,.

God provides us with everything we need and more if we simply ask and turn to him. Next time you find yourself in need, remember God is always there and ready to equip you with whatever you need.

Jesus replied, 'What is impossible with men is possible with God.'

Luke 18:27 (NIV)

Our God is almighty, he can do anything, he is in control of our lives and he understands everything we are going through. There is nothing that God cannot do and sometimes the only person that can help us is God. Learn to look to him for help when things look impossible, because he is the only one who can make a difference.

But the fruit of the Spirit is love, joy, peace, patience, kindness, goodness, faithfulness, gentleness and self-control.

Galatians 5:22-23 (NIV)

The 'fruits of the spirit' are things God would like us to have, almost like our '5-a-day'. These are characteristics we should try to develop to help us live a life that is pleasing to him. God tells us that if we ask then he will provide.

So next time you are in difficulty, stop, and ask God to equip you to deal with the situation, the chances are you'll need to top up on your fruit of the spirit.

In all your ways acknowledge him, and he will make your paths straight.

Proverbs 3:6 (NIV)

Ever wondered what will happen tomorrow, how that exam will go, what job you will get, who you are going to marry? God knows the answer to all these questions. God is omniscient, this means all seeing, all knowing, and he knows everything about your life, where you have been and where you are going. Often we can try to control our lives and decide our future. We forget that God is there to help and guide us. When we become Christians we give our lives to God, this means acknowledging that he has a plan for us.

Look to God for guidance and if you lose your way, ask and he will put you back on the straight and narrow.

May the God of hope fill you with all joy and peace as you trust in him, so that you may overflow with hope by the power of the Holy Spirit.

Romans 15:13 (NIV)

Hope is a word often used in the bible and this verse stresses that the hope we have in God is certain hope not hoping for something that may never happen. So often we hope for things that never materialise and it can leave us feeling let down and disappointed. This verse is telling us that the hope we can have in God is different and this will fill us with joy and peace and make us overflow.

Have hope in God and his plan for you, and be exited.

I have good plans for you, not plans to hurt you. I will give you hope and a good future.
Jeremiah 29:11 9 (NCV)

God's plans are brilliant, amazing, better than we can imagine. To fulfil God's plan for our life, we need to trust him to guide us. God's plans aren't often how we would plan, but he loves us and wants the very best for us. We can to turn to him to guide us, and trust him when he leads us.

So we do not give up. Our physical body is becoming older and weaker, but our spirit inside us is made new every day.

2 Corinthians 4:16 (NCV)

Everywhere we look there are products, clothes, food brands and adverts to get 'the perfect body'. The world today has become so fixated on how we look, that it can be difficult to remember that our bodies don't last forever. Our bodies are not permanent; when we enter heaven we are all given new shining bodies.

So even though it is important to look after our bodies, don't let it rule your life because your spirit inside is what will stay with you forever.

What good is it for a man to gain the whole world, yet forfeit his soul?

Mark 8:36 (NIV)

If all your possessions, family and friends were taken away from you, what would you have left? Do you have a relationship with God, can you rely on him like a best friend, do you love him like your partner, and can you take advice from him like a teacher?

Your relationship with God needs to be the most important thing you have. It can be hard to build a relationship with someone we cannot see, but that doesn't mean you can't. Dedicate your time to getting to know God, spending time with him, learning to trust and follow him.

It is great to have friends, family and nice possessions, but when they are taken away what would be left?

We have small troubles for a while now, but they are helping us gain an eternal glory that is much greater than the troubles. We set our eyes not on what we see but on what we cannot see. What we see will last only a short time, but what we cannot see will last forever.

2 Corinthians 4:17-18 (NCV)

It is hard to remember that our life on earth is not permanent, it's only temporary, and somewhere we are passing through before moving on to heaven.

We all lead busy lives which in turn can make us tired, and in the busyness of life we can lose perspective. Even though you are busy, remember to look beyond today, have an eternal perspective, not only do you have an exciting future ahead of you, but you have a life in heaven that will far outweigh our lives today.

Made in the USA
Monee, IL
04 November 2026

67377190R00036